# SPIRITS
# &
# EAGLES

A glimpse at Lakota life and traditions

on Cheyenne River Sioux Reservation, SD.

Tricia Sedivy

*Chan te' was te' wen*

Copyright © February, 2003
By Patricia Sedivy
All Rights Reserved

No part of this book may be reproduced, stored in a retrievable system, or transmitted by any means, electronic, photocopying, recording, or otherwise, without written permission from the author.

Printed in the United States of America

Published by

Book Surge, LLC
5341 Dorchester Rd., Suite 16
No. Charleston, SC 29418

Photos by:
Tricia and Joe Sedivy
All photos taken with permission.

***"Spirits & Eagles"*** is the true story of how meeting a nine year old Lakota girl resulted in the writer's discovery of a spiritual connection of her past to the present and being adopted by Romanus Bear Stops who lives on Cheyenne River Sioux Reservation, SD.

What is a *sweat lodge ceremony*? What is the significance of the numbers 4 & 7? Why are the flesh offerings given at a *Sun Dance* not barbaric?

*"The dense cloud seemed to wrap around me, just like being in a "sweat. I could hear Romanus praying, Gloria and others singing ...."*

*".... we have a Third World country right here in the United States!"*

## THE CIRCLE OF LIFE

Indian people have very strong ties to the earth. It is their Mother. They hold sacred all plants, creatures, all that is created.

The Circle of Life is central to the culture of the Plains Indians. Although the names and symbols differ (The Sacred hoop, Medicine Wheel, The Sacred Circle, Circle of Life), the belief is that all life revolves in a circle, an endless loop tied to the natural spiritual world.

The circle is divided into four directions, with each direction signifying a different spirit, power, color and animal from which strength can be drawn.

In this way, the People say that all is related. The Lakota say " Mitakaye Oyasin ... All my relations."

LENA SITTING CROW
JUNE, 1991

Dedicated to Lena Sitting Crow who brought me to Cheyenne River Sioux Reservation, SD, where I found….

Family….

Friends…

Myself…

## *ACKNOWLEDGMENTS*

Without the support of family members and friends, this book may not have been written. Special thanks to:

Joe, my husband… thank you for your encouragement, patience, and believing I could write this.
I love you. (Y.L.U.M.L.)

My parents, Tom and Oma McQuay ... (I have seen Dad's smiling face in the clouds while at Sun Dance.) You always believed I could accomplish anything I set my mind to. You helped me to believe in myself.

Tom Rome, my son…never let your belief in the Sun Dance and involvement with our family and friends in Red Scaffold fade.

Mary Jo Peer, my longtime friend… Thank you for your friendship and the many experiences we have shared.

Romanus Bear Stops… I am honored to call you "Father". Thank you for your love and all you continue to teach me.

Gloria & Vernel Sitting Crow…my Lakota brother and sister. There are no words to express what you mean to me.

Zona Bear Stops... I know you are watching over me. I miss hearing the stories of your life and I treasure the Sun Dance shawl you gave me for my first Sun Dance.

Molly Circle Bear... I miss your remarks like, " You are like the eagle. We never know when or where you will land or how long you will stay."

Germaine Sitting Crow ...thank you for your guidance at Sun Dance and the beaded lighter. I love your smile.

Catherine, Teresa, Marie, Marlene, Connie, and all the Sun Dancers... thank you for your prayers, patience and understanding as you taught me about Sun Dance and Lakota traditions.

Byram Fire Department, Byram NJ; Ed and Ann Rogalsky, Lila Wainer, Heather Koenigsburg, Sammy Rabin, people of Byram Township. Stanhope, Andover, Newton, Netcong, Sparta, NJ, host families, and many others ... thank you for your generosity and continued support of the people living in Red Scaffold.

Thanks to Dr. Tirpak and Dr. Sullivan, Sparta, NJ,

for taking care of those with dental needs, and to
Dr. Casella, Byram Township, NJ, for medical needs.

Youth Connection and people of Andover
Presbyterian Church, Andover NJ...thank you
for the annual Christmas Toy Drive and other donations for those living on Cheyenne River Sioux Reservation,SD. For some children, this is the only Christmas gift they receive.

Barbara Levens, a dear friend ... without your computer help, this book would not have been written. God Bless!

The people of Red Scaffold...thank you for your love, acceptance, and understanding

Most of all, I thank the Great Spirit for bringing Lena Sitting Crow into my life.

*We do not want riches.
We want peace and love."*

Red Cloud (1870)

*" ... we are bound ...*
*to watch out for*
*each other's preservation ... "*


CANASSATEGO  1742

# Contents

| | |
|---|---|
| Acknowledgments | 10 |
| The Spirits Speak | 16 |
| Preface | 18 |
| My Adoption | 23 |
| Lena Sitting Crow | 24 |
| I Visit Lena | 30 |
| The Tourist Route | 39 |
| Reservation Communities | 43 |
| My First Inipi | 48 |
| Our Last Night | 55 |
| Answers | 58 |
| Power of Prayer | 65 |
| Another Visit to the Reservation | 71 |
| Eagles | 80 |
| Religion & Wiwanyag Wachipi | |
| (Sun Dance) | 88 |
| My First Sun Dance | 95 |
| Healing Ceremony | 102 |
| Flesh Offering | 104 |
| Visits to New Jersey | 108 |
| Returning for Sun Dance | 118 |
| Dancing at Sun Dance | 124 |
| And Now | 131 |
| Update | 134 |
| A Special Gift | 139 |
| About the Author | 151 |
| Bibliography | 152 |
| More Information | 154 |

**The Spirits Speak ...**

> My heart aches
> > For those I have not met.
>
> My eyes tear
> > For those only my mind sees.
>
> My ears hear
> > The crying of the
> > > spirits from the past.
>
> My mind understands
> > That which I do not know.
>
> I look to the sky and see
> > The eagle that is not there.
>
> **The Spirits speak ...**
>
> > **The Eagle guides me ...**

## *PREFACE ..*

Cheyenne River Sioux Reservation, SD, is a two hour drive northeast of Rapid City. The over 2,800,00 acres (about the size of Connecticut) is home to over 14,000 Lakota Indians. For the past twelve years, I have been visiting Red Scaffold, a small reservation community 20 miles from the town of Faith.

I wrote the first draft of this book (originally titled "Guided by the Eagle") six years ago. I knew the manuscript wasn't complete. I believed the Great Spirit would let me know when the time was right to finish it. Unable to be at Sun Dance this year (June, 2002), I was really feeling low when I thought of the manuscript. As I removed the file from the cabinet drawer, a warm excitement flowed through me. I began reading. I knew it was time for me to complete the story of my adoption by Romanus Bear Stops and my connection with the Sitting Crow family.

I sat down at the computer and began the rewrite and update. The words flowed as if someone were whispering in my ear, telling me what to write. Over the years, I have learned to listen to these "inner" voices and feelings.

Before you read on, I'd like to share one of many incidents I have experienced since meeting Lena Sitting Crow.

Due to an upper respiratory infection in June 2001,

I almost didn't go to Sun Dance. A week before
I was scheduled to fly to Rapid City, the doctor wanted
to put me in the hospital. I convinced him (and my
husband) to give me another 24 hours. I didn't know
why I needed the time; I just knew that I did.

My upstairs bedroom has three regular walls. The
fourth wall is a divider holding a dozen assorted plants.

When in bed, I face the divider. Before getting in
bed that night, I arranged my pillows so I could sleep
sitting upright. It was 1220 am before I was finally
situated in the bed. I began to doze. Around 1 am,
I thought I heard someone call my name. I opened
my eyes and listened. Nothing.

This happened several times before I saw the "eyes"
in the plants.

Looking directly at me was a pair of piercing red eyes.
(I had seen those eyes before.) A haze appeared to
be rising from my body, similar to the haze seen
rising from a blacktopped road on a hot, sunny day.
I thought I was dreaming. The haze became
so dense, I could not see the plants, only those
piercing, compassionate eyes staring at me. I reached
over to touch Joe lying beside me. He was sound
asleep.

This dense cloud seemed to wrap around me, just
like being in a "sweat" on the reservation.

I could hear Romanus praying; Gloria and several others singing. The comforting, misty cloud slowly disappeared. After looking at the clock , I quickly fell asleep. It was 2:40 am.

I had been sleeping upright for two weeks. Imagine my surprise when I awoke that morning and realized I had slept all night lying my on stomach.

Romanus and Gloria knew I was very sick and may not be at Sun Dance. I wasn't surprised when she called me that morning to see I how was feeling. I told her what had happened and that I was feeling a lot better. That's when she told me Romanus had held a " healing sweat " for me around 10 PM. New Jersey time is two hours ahead of South Dakota. That meant they were all in the " sweat " when I saw the eyes and was engulfed by the healing cloud.

They knew I would be OK.

The Great Spirit was watching over me. ( I did go to Sun Dance.)

*" Have a vision
not clouded by fear. "*

The Cherokee

*" We are a part of the earth,
and the earth
is a part of us."*

## CHIEF SEATTLE

## MY ADOPTION...

I stand on a bed of sage at the foot of the Sun Dance tree, looking up at the sky. A hand stitched quilt, made by Molly Circle Bear, is wrapped around my shoulders. Romanus Bear Stops stands to my left, praying in Lakota, asking the Great Spirit to bless the eagle feathers that will be placed in my hair. Roy Circle Bear stands to my right. Zona Bear Stops is behind me.

We turn to pay homage to the four directions ... the east, the south, the west, the north.

They are all praying in Lakota.

All the while, I am praying to be worthy of this honor.

"Please guide me in whatever direction You have planned for me. Help me to understand what it is I am to do. Let my new family and friends always know how much I love them."

The chorus of a church hymn plays in my mind,.

"Here I am Lord ... Is it I Lord ... I have heard you calling in the night ... I will go Lord ... if you lead me ... I will hold your people in my heart."

*Memories of the past flood my mind ...*

# LENA SITTING CROW

I first met Lena Sitting Crow, a young Sioux Indian girl, in July, 1990. She was "almost 10". Lena had the long black, silky hair we expect of Native American children. Her eyes, as dark as obsidian, were hypnotizing. At that time, I had no idea the impact she and her family would have on my life.

Lena came to New Jersey with a group from Cheyenne River Sioux Reservation, SD. Twenty-eight, mostly children, had traveled 36 hours on a school bus to visit people they did not know who lived in a part of the country they had never seen. Lena was the last child on the bus because her parents were very unsure about allowing her to go. Gloria Sitting Crow, Lena's mother, thought there was an unknown reason for Lena to visit New Jersey. She " felt " Lena was supposed to go.

When they arrived in New Jersey, I boarded the bus to greet our visitors. Most of these children had never been away from their reservation. I was introducing them to their host families when I discovered I had a "shadow". One of the younger girls had attached herself to me. When she asked who was staying with me, I told her no one. We were doing some remodeling at our home and I was not going to be hosting any of our guests.

I overheard her telling two of the other girls that she was "going home with Trish ". I tried to explain about the renovation being done at my house and that the steps to the upstairs were torn out. I looked into her eyes and saw trust and love. We experienced an instant connection. You guessed it; she went home with me.

After we went home, I decided to take her shopping for a bathing suit. I wrote a note for Joe, my husband, letting him know Lena would be staying with us. Tom, our son, stopped by the house while we were gone. He didn't see my note to Joe when he turned the piece of paper over to write me a note. Joe didn't see my note when he came home.

Looking out our kitchen window, Joe saw me entering the yard with this little girl. Being the great guy he is, he said, "Looks like we have a visitor. How long can we keep her? "

Lena was a little shy around most people, but never with me. In the beginning, Joe often asked me if Lena could talk. He would ask her a question and she would nod her head or shrug her shoulders. By the end of the week, this changed a little. She would answer "yes", "no", or shrug her shoulders. She was always polite.

When we went shopping, she never asked for anything. When I gave her spending money, she usually spent it on gifts for one of her brothers or sisters.

Lena has two brothers and three sisters. Her family is traditional Sioux. All perform at reservation powwows. The family's religious and spiritual beliefs are centered on the Great Spirit, Sweat Lodge ceremonies, and the Sun Dance. Her grandparents, Romanus and Zona Bear Stops, Germaine Sitting Crow, and Roy and Molly Circle Bear, speak Lakota, the language of the Sioux. Lena is proud of her family and her heritage. Little did I know how intertwined our lives would become.

While the group was here, they wanted to visit the Statue of Liberty, which we arranged. We took them to Action Park, a water park in Vernon, NJ , and swimming at Sandy Hook, a New Jersey Federal Park with beaches on the Atlantic Ocean. Many had never seen the ocean. They were amazed at the vastness and the salty taste
of the water.

During Lena's first visit, she explained many of her customs, and ceremonies. For some unknown reason, I was able to relate to what she was saying. It was as if I had participated in these rituals. But, that wasn't possible. Was it? Or , was it memories of stories about the Cherokees told to me as a child by family and friends when I visited them in the Smoky Mountains of Tennessee?

I have always wondered if the body is just a vessel for our soul. When the body dies, can the soul can be reborn in another body? If so, could I have been an Indian in another life?

One of the rituals Lena promised I would be able to experience when I visited her was the *Inipi* (sweat lodge). She spent hours teaching me the correct pronunciation of *" Mitakuye Oyasin "* (All my relations) which is said when entering and leaving the sweat lodge, at the end of a prayer, and when you want the sweat lodge entrance flap opened. After a lot of practicing, I finally, got it .......
" *Me-dak-e-ay-see. Me-dak-e-ay-see* ".

We spent hours talking about her family, traditions, life on the reservation, her school, what she liked and disliked. This entrancing young girl and I became very close. There were times when I looked into her eyes and felt as if I was being drawn into another life, a missing fragmentof my life as I know it. To this day, there is a special bond between us that time and distance does not diminish. When she left, I felt as if I was saying good-bye one of my own children. A few days after Lena left, I was looking for information in my computer and discovered a message from her:

" Rember
>I know we'll meet again know matter
> the distance.
>Between..
>Remember the old time's the
>> memories we've seen, the
>> other's will come and leaving

>> Laughter and tear's thinking of past
>> time's now called wouder year's
>> But I kno you cann't hide

> The feeling's of renber, when now
>> scool day's are forgotten, knew life
>> begans with Brand new loveing
>> memories, brand new rember when's
>> Just keep my friendshipin your heart

> For advise now and thenfor when you
>> open your eye's
>> I'll be there for you each day."

Her words brought tears to my eyes and joy to my heart! Even today, whenever I'm feeling down, I read her message and it makes me happier.

My heritage is Cherokee (and Irish). Often, I have wondered if the Great Spirit (Kanati in Cherokee, Wakan T'anka in Sioux), God, destiny (or, whatever you call the Supreme Being) planned the coming together of the Sitting Crow family and myself? Are we bound together by a spiritual ribbon of our ancestors?

History tells of many Cherokees joining the Sioux when they were forced to leave their homes in 1838-39 (" the trail of tears " ; or, as the Cherokee's say " the trail where they wept ". ) Is that our connection? Are our minds similar to computers with memory chips? Do we pass on memories from generation to generation? If so, could there be a genetic link between the Sitting Crow family and myself?

*" I love a people who have always made me welcome to the best they had ... who are honest without laws ... who never takes the name of God in vain ... who worships God without a Bible ... and I believe God loves them."*

George Catlin
Artist, 1830

# I VISIT LENA

A month later, I visited Lena and her family who live in the reservation community of Red Scaffold. Twenty of us, including Joe and several other adults and children from our area, flew to South Dakota.

We were excited when the plane took off from Newark airport. As our connecting flight departed Denver for Rapid City, my own apprehension and anticipation of the unknown grew. We were flying over the barren plains when, in the distance, there were green trees…. the famous Black Hills of South Dakota. The sight sent chills down my spine.

A calming excitement, a feeling of "going home" came over me. I had never been to South Dakota. Where did this sensation come from? Since then, I have returned many times and these emotions are always the same.

When our plane landed in Rapid City that first trip, I could hardly speak. (Very unusual for me.) I felt as if something unexpected, exciting and unexplainable was about to happen. I wasn't disappointed!

Joe and I were looking forward to meeting Lena's family and the other host families who lived on the reservation. We were greeted at the Rapid City airport by several of the adults who chaperoned the group to New Jersey.

On the way to Cheyenne River Sioux Reservation (two hours away), we stopped at a small homestead at the foot of Bear Butte. Bear Butte is a sacred mountain where Native Americans of many tribes go to pray to the Great Spirit. Members of Tribal Council presented the organization a Cheyenne River Sioux Reservation flag.

Afterwards, we boarded the bus and continued the drive to the reservation. Looking out of the bus windows, most of us watched the passing scenery in silence. We were used to the mountainous "green" of northern New Jersey. We were unable to relate to the dry, barren, flat landscape.

During this first visit, the weather was extremely dry due to a six-year drought. The Cheyenne River was very low and a few of its tributaries were dry. The hard, dry ground had deep cracks and crevices that made walking treacherous in some areas. Even dry and barren, the beauty of the land in this area could not be denied. You could feel the spirituality of Mother Earth.

Because of an annual powwow on the Lower Brule Reservation, several of our host families would not be home till the next day. We doubled up in a few of the host homes. Sitting outside that night, we marveled at the magnificent clear night sky. Millions of stars in the dark, velvet sky appeared close enough to touch. Every few minutes an abrupt burst of lightning would illuminate the sky as if Father Sky was trying to show us a glimpse of heaven. It was breathtaking! We were as excited as little kids on Christmas Eve.

The next morning we experienced our first "official" Indian powwow. Arrangements had been made by the Supervisor at Takini , the reservation school, for us to travel by school bus to the Lower Brule powwow. This is when we learned about "Indian time".

After several members of our group asked me how long the ride was going to be, I asked our driver. At first, he said he didn't know, he was going to "time it this trip'. I asked him how long it normally took him to drive from his home to Lower Bruele.

He replied, " Four cigarettes." (It took about two hours.)

We knew Lena was dancing and her family was at the powwow. When we arrived, I went looking for Gloria and Vernel, her parents. I had no idea what they looked like; but, knew Vernel sang and played the drum. Seeing four groups of singers and dancers outside the performance circle, I trotted off to find Vernel. Approaching each group, I knew I was being watched. Vernel was with the last group. He knew who I was as soon as I said his name. Immediately, he stood up and hugged me. It was like discovering a long lost brother! We weren't able to do much talking because he was performing. (We made up for it later.) Others watched with confusion, wondering who is that *wasicu* (whiteman/woman)? He pointed to Gloria sitting in the bleachers with Justin, Lena's 18 month old brother.

When Gloria saw me, there was acceptance, love, and understanding in her eyes. Justin, a chunky little guy with "chipmunk cheeks', big dark eyes, and black, silky hair sat on her lap. When I said "hi" to him, he held out his little arms and came to me without crying.

My oldest daughter is only four years younger than Gloria, but we have no "age gap". We sat and talked while waiting for the other children.

Gloria and her family believe and live their heritage. They realize the importance of an education and the need for their children to learn about life away from the reservation. With all the obstacles they have had to overcome, Vernel and Gloria finished high school and attended college.

Gloria has over 100 college credits and worked for

minimum wage establishing and supervising youth education programs underwritten by H.U.D. Funds for this program were cancelled and there is no longer a funded youth program. She now drives an hour each morning, over several dirt roads, to Eagle Butte where she works for Head Start.

Vernel drives a Head Start school bus and assists in coordinating youth basketball tournaments between reservation communities. He and Gloria are both actively involved with their community and highly respected by their people.

It wasn't long before Lena's two younger sisters came to meet the *wasicu* talking to their Mom. LaRee, petite and shy, was six years old. Outspoken CherRon was four. Both gave me a hug as they softly said, "Hi Trish."

The powwow was more informal and less commercialized than those I had attended in the northeast. Joe and I were impressed by the powwow opening ceremony.

The American flag was raised on a pole in the center of the arbor (performance circle) as a special prayer was sung to the Great Spirit. There were tears in my eyes as I watched the flag moving slowly to the top of the pole.

It was then that I noticed the American flag topped all the poles of the arbor. The first to enter the circle were the veterans of the U.S. Military, followed by the procession of performers. Its hard to comprehend their loyalty to a government that has treated them so badly. (i.e., In violation of the Treaty of 1868, hundreds of their ancestors, mostly women and children, were massacred at Wounded Knee, Pine Ridge Reservation, SD, by U.S. Army soldiers, Dec. 29, 1890. They were buried there in a mass grave.)

The dancing began. My feet were tapping to the beat when I heard myself humming with the music. At the time, I thought it was because of similarity to music heard elsewhere. Now I wonder if this was my first connection to my lost heritage.

I saw Lena (a champion jingle dancer) dancing. As I watched her, our eyes met. That same rapport was there. Time and miles had not changed anything. She still had a special aura about her. Seeing her in her native environment, I knew she was a special child and our lives would always be connected.

We welcomed the warm greetings and friendliness of our new friends. Our group enjoyed the day devouring Indian tacos and fry bread, buying handmade crafts, gorgeous star quilts, beaded jewelry and belt buckles. One of the boys bought a skinned, red fox that he was able to manipulate like hand puppet. We now had a mascot.

I didn't want the day to end. All day, I had enjoyed a comfortable "at home" feeling.

> " *Might I behold thee,*
> *Might I know thee,*
> *Might I consider thee,*
> *Might I understand thee,*
> *One Lord of the Universe.* "

INCA SONG

LENA SITTING CROW
&
TRICIA

*" That hand is not the color
of your hand,
but if I pierce it, I shall feel pain.
The blood that will follow from mine
will be the same color as yours.
The Great Spirit made us both."*

STANDING BEAR

## THE TOURIST ROUTE

The following day, our group did the tourist route: Badlands, Crazy Horse Monument, site of the Wounded Knee Massacre, and Mt. Rushmore.

The Badlands were awesome! Looking down into the dunes and buttes, you knew they had been aptly named. These wondrous hills had been the hideout for many outlaws of the old west and refuge for many Indians. I could envision Indians riding bareback on Pinto ponies, hiding in a crevice, laughing when *wasicus* (whitemen) got lost trying to find them.

Crazy Horse is considered to be one of the greatest Sioux Chiefs because he would not give in to the "whitemanizing" demanded of his people by the U.S. Government. He never signed an agreement to have his people live on a reservation.

According to the Sioux, Crazy Horse never wanted war. He just wanted to save his people. He fought back when the *wasicus* entered Sioux land and began killing his people. Crazy Horse was killed (Sept. 5, 1877) by an Army solder, after being tricked into going to Nebraska's Fort Robinson for a council with U.S. government representatives. It is said, his bodywas secretly buried somewhere in the Badlands.

"My fellow chiefs and I would like the white man to know the red man had many great leaders, too.", wrote Henry Standing Bear (in 1947) when he invited German sculptor Korczak Ziolkowski to come to the Black Hills to carve a monument to Crazy Horse. Korczak accepted his invitation. Work on the monument began in 1949 and is still being sculpted by family members.

When completed, this monument will be 563 feet high, 641 feet long, and taller then the Washington Monument. All four heads of Mt. Rushmore would fit inside the head of the Crazy Horse monument. Four thousand people could stand on the out stretched arm (almost as long as a football field). A 10-story building would fit under his arm. The head of his horse will be 22 stories tall. This tribute to Crazy Horse is being constructed entirely without federal or state aid. The monument, not far from Mt. Rushmore, is a nonprofit " cultural and educational memorial to the Indians of North America". (According to the Crazy Horse Monument brochure.)

When I first saw Mt. Rushmore, I thought, " This does not belong here. The Black Hills are sacred grounds. It's an insult to Native Americans to flaunt these sculptures of Presidents who did nothing to help the Indians."

Sioux friends told me to look toward the left and I would see the profile of an Indian. Black Elk, an Oglala Sioux Holy Man, said he would appear there after death. And, you know? They're right! He is there!

Our group was allowed to visit a small Sun Dance ceremony on Pine Ridge Reservation (near the Badlands). Women had to wear long skirts. Those women " in their time of the moon" (menstruating) had to stay away from the sacred circle and the dancers. (It is believed these women may rob the dancers of their strength.) Men could not wear hats. Taking of photographs was not allowed.

Once again, I had that feeling of de'ja'vu. I understood the religious significance as I watched the piercing of the dancers. Why did I understand? How was I able to accept and understand something I thought I knew nothing about?

The following year, Joe and I were guests of the Sitting Crow family at the Bear Stops Sun Dance in Red Scaffold. (I'll explain about Sun Dance later.)

*" I know every stream
and every wood ...
like my fathers before me.
I live happily"*


TEN BEARS

# RESERVATION COMMUNITIES

The next day we visited several reservation communities: Cherry Creek, Bridger, and Red Scaffold (Lena's home).

We were outraged when the reservation doctor showed us a sterilizer that had been broken for five years. He told of never having more than four suture kits and he must divide his time between the communities, all with ill equipped clinics.

There are huge aluminum buildings constructed years ago by the U.S. Government to house fire trucks and ambulances that never came. The closest fire department is in Eagle Butte, an hour away. The closest hospital is in Rapid City, a two hour drive from the reservation. Fire hydrants are in several reservation communities, but there are no fire hoses Knowing they will never see emergency equipment in these structures, the large open buildings are used for basketball games and community events.

The following winter, the home of an elderly woman in Cherry Creek was destroyed by fire and two children suffered burns. I was told that a fire hydrant was only 50 feet from their home. Not having fire hoses, they were unable to contain or put out the fire. Joe is a volunteer fireman and could not accept this. He decided to try to get fire hoses for Red Scaffold and other reservation communities.

In Cherry Creek, we saw women doing laundry at an artisan well. They filled five-gallon buckets with soap and water, then washed the clothes by hand. Another bucket was filled with water to rinse the items. Children were stomping their feet in the buckets to clean and rinse the clothes. They looked like they were stomping grapes for wine. The scene reminded me of pictures I have seen of life in some Third World Countries. This is when I realized we have a Third World Country right here in the United States!

There are other Native American reservations even more destitute then Cheyenne River.

When compared to other Americans, many people feel Native Americans living on reservations have very little. How wrong they are. The pride and family values expressed by the people of Cheyenne River Sioux Reservation is seldom seen in American homes.

That evening we moved to Red Scaffold and into the Sitting Crow's small ranch style home. The center of Red Scaffold is one road, less than a mile long. Approximately 25 families live in this area. Red Scaffold is not as flat as other areas of the reservation, having several buttes and hills. Horses are often seen grazing in the open plains and by the roadside. At the bottom of the main street were trailers, a gym (one of the aluminum buildings I mentioned earlier) and the clinic (the doctor is there one day, every two weeks)  There was an artisan well near a polluted stream that spills water on the debris lying on the ground. An old one-room church, not used much anymore, several vacant uninhabitable houses and trailers, an old Head Start building (classes were moved to any empty house up the street) complete the center of this community. A small Catholic church is on the main road.

The closest grocery store is in Faith, 20 miles away. When we entered the Sitting Crow home, the first thing I saw was a life size warrior on horseback, painted in shades of blue, on the living room wall. This was my first glimpse of Vernel's exceptional artistic abilities.

The sparsely furnished home was clean and very comfortable. A small TV fussily received two stations. There was a VCR, sofa and chair. One or two beds was in each of the three bedrooms. There were no bureaus or cabinets . A combination kitchen/ dining area, with a table and four chairs, was behind the living room.

Joe and I had boxes of groceries and "goodies" for the family. The Sitting Crow children were excited and invited their friends to meet Lena's " New Jersey Mom ".   (I explained to LaRee and CherRon, Lena has only one Mom. I am a special friend.)

As excited as the children were they all shared their "goodies" with their friends. Never once, did we hear "That's mine". When only one small container of juice was left, LeRee offered it to one of her friends.

Everyone in the community shares with one another. They watch over one each others children; respect and take care of their elderly, and share food and clothing. The more I learned, the more I wanted to know, and the more " at home " I felt.

When it was time for bed, Joe and I were given the bedroom shared by Lena, LaRee and CherRon. The next morning, we realized Lena and her sisters had slept tripled up in a bed in another room. Gloria and Vernel slept with Justin on a piece of foam rubber on the living room floor. I asked the whereabouts of Troy (Lena's 11 year old brother) and Jennifer (her 15 year old sister). Troy was staying in Vermillion (three hours away) with Germaine Sitting Crow, his grandmother. Jennifer was staying with another relative. This was done to make room for us.

*"Too many misinterpretations
have been made....
Too many misunderstandings...*

Chief Joseph

# MY FIRST INIPI
## *(Sweat Lodge Ceremony)*

An *Inipi* (Sweat Lodge Ceremony) was planned at Takini School for our group's participation. There was to be one for the women and one for the men. I was told coed "sweats" were only for families and special friends. I was surprised when Gloria told me I couldn't go to Takini. Then she said her father, Romanus Bear Stops, wanted me at their family "sweat" that evening! He would conduct the " sweat " in the Red Scaffold community lodge. I was elated and felt very,very honored.

Explaining the religious significance of the *Inipi* may help you to understand its spirituality.

The sweat lodge is made of saplings (usually willow) bent and tied together with twine to form a dome-shaped hogan, eight to twelve feet in diameter. Years ago, buffalo robes and animal hides were used to cover the lodge. Today, the lodge is covered with tarps or blankets. The entrance always faces east, towards the rising sun. In the center of the lodge, representing the center of the universe, a pit is dug to hold heated, sacred rocks. The rocks symbolize Mother Earth and Wakan T'anka, the Great Spirit.

The fire heats the sacred rocks and is symbolic of

the great power of Wakan T'anka who gives life to all living things. Sage is spread on the floor. (If you have trouble breathing during the ceremony because of the intense heat, place the sage in your cupped hands and hold under your nose. Take deep breaths, breathing in the aroma of the sage.)

There is a sacred path from the pit outside the lodge to a small mound of dirt in front of the sacred fire where the rocks are heated. (Lena told me not to walk across the sacred path, walk around it. You only walk on the path when entering and leaving the lodge.)

The sacred fire represents the eternal flame within the center of the universe. The red-hot rocks symbolize the creator. A traditional pipe (often called a "peace pipe") is filled with tobacco, usually mixed with red cedar or sage. After the pipe is filled, it is placed on the mound. (As far as I know peyote, used in ceremonies by some members of the Native American Church, is not used by those living in Red Scaffold.)

Someone, usually a woman (representative of the Buffalo Calf woman who gave the Sioux their sacred pipe), circles the sacred fire clockwise, dropping grains of tobacco into the fire. The lodge can now be entered.

Men wear shorts or only a towel wrapped around

their waists. Women wear a long skirt, tee shirt, and no undergarments. You enter the lodge on your hands and knees as you say " *Matakuye Oyasin* " (" All my relations "), crawls to the left side of the lodge and sit in front of the pit that will hold the sacred rocks. The ceremony leader enters last and sits by the entrance. A bucket of water and ladle are placed beside the ceremony leader.

The fire tender (outside the lodge) begins carrying the red-hot sacred rocks (using a pitchfork or shovel) to the lodge, dropping them into the pit inside the lodge. Grains of tobacco are dropped on each rock. Antlers are used to turn and move the rocks. When all the sacred rocks have been placed in the pit, the door flap is dropped over the lodge entrance. You are in total darkness.

The ceremony leader welcomes everyone and begins praying to Wakan T'anka, Mother Earth, Father Sky, and the four directions. During this time, water is being ladled onto the sacred rocks in the pit, creating the feeling of being in a steamy sauna.
As the heat intensifies, you begin to sweat. It is believed your sweat joins with that of the others in the lodge and intermingles with the steam from the sacred rocks. Combined, all become one.

This sacred blending will be carried to the four corners of the world and apart of you will seep back into Mother Earth.

If the heat is too much for you, say *"Mitakuye Oyasin"* and the entrance flap will be opened. During the ceremony, the entrance can only be opened four times, once for each of the four directions.

The person sitting to the left of the ceremony leader begins praying out loud. When they finish praying, the next person prays, then the next, until everyone has prayed. If you do not wish to pray aloud, you say *" Mitakuye Oyasin"*. There is singing between the prayers.

My first *inipi* was hypnotizing, revealing, exciting, and frightening. I had read stories about people seeing visions, hearing voices, and having psychic experiences when in a "sweat". I never thought it could happen to me.

Preparing for the *inipi*, I was overcome with mixed emotions, questions, and uncertainties. Would I remember everything Lena told me? What if I did or said something wrong? How long would it last? Could I endure the intense heat? Romanus had just met me. Why was I invited to participate in their family sweat?

Silently, I kept repeating, " *Me-dak-e-ay-see ... Me-dak-e-ay-see ... Me-dak-e-ay-see ... Me-dak-e-ay-see ...*"

It was time to enter the lodge.

Entering the sacred structure on my hands and knees, all my apprehensions disappeared. I remembered to say " *Mitakuye Oyasin* ". Sitting with my legs crossed, I was transported to another world . The fire tender began placing the sacred rocks in the pit.

During the ceremony, I was oblivious to the intense heat. Romanus, speaking in Lakota then in English, thanked me for taking care Lena, of his grand daughter, when she visited New Jersey .

Tears rolled down my cheeks as he welcomed me to their family. Seldom have I ever felt such love and acceptance.

Each time someone said "*Mitakuye Oyasin* " to have the door flap opened, I saw the fire (adjacent to the lodge) where the sacred rocks were heated. I was hypnotized by the face of a young girl, then a profile of a noble looking Indian, followed by two animal like eyes that my mind saw in the flames.

In the darkness of the lodge, I heard myself singing with the others. I felt several light touches on my right cheek, like the brushing of a feathery plume.
I could feel the love, pain, hope, understanding, acceptance, wants and needs of these extraordinary people.

Afterwards, I was so shaken I didn't know if I

should speak about my experiences or what I saw in the flames. I was confused, yet calm. Somewhere, deep inside me, I knew I had connected with my Indian heritage.

Gloria said, "It was a good sweat. The presence of the spirits was very strong."

When we got back to the house, I decided to tell Gloria and Vernel what I had seen and felt while in the "sweat". (Vernel and Joe had stayed home with the younger children.)

Gloria and Vernel told me the spirits had recognized me as being a "good person, pure of heart".

They did not know the meaning of the faces or eyes I had seen in the fire or who the may represent.

Having an analytical mind, Joe was not sure what to think. Fortunately, he does believe things can happen that cannot be rationalized. Listening to me talk, he knew I had experienced something very spiritual and meaningful.

I am grateful for his understanding and acceptance because meeting Lena Sitting Crow and her family has had a pronounced effect on what I feel, think, and do in my life today.

After participating in an *inipi*, there is a feeling of being reborn. You know, without a doubt, you can handle whatever life has in store for you. You are not alone!

The Great Spirit (God), a very powerful and supportive force, is watching over you. He will provide you with the strength and understanding needed to face all of life's trials and tribulations.

An *inipi* must be personally experienced in order to comprehend the spirituality and feeling of "oneness" with the universe. There is no way to describe this overwhelming feeling. It can only be experienced.

*" Friend and brother: It was the will of the Great Spirit that we should meet together this day."*

## SITTING BULL

# OUR LAST NIGHT

Our last night arrived too soon. We were all invited to the Red Scaffold community powpow. There would be a "potluck" dinner and the opportunity to see many of new friends performing their traditional dances.

Before the festivities, our group was given paper plates, cups, and plastic spoons. We were asked to get in line to eat. There was a delicious stew, potato salad, Jello, fry bread and Kool-aid. (Joe and I loved the fry bread.)

The dancers, toddlers to adults, were competing for prizes. Watching the dancers adorned in their traditional attire, listening to the singing and the beat of the drums, I was totally entranced.

Abruptly, I was brought back to reality when I heard, " Will Joe and Tricia Sedivy please step into the center of the circle!"

Where's Joe?

Again, "Will Tricia and Joe Sedivy please step into the center of the circle!"

There's Joe!

Relunctantly, entering the dance circle, we saw Gloria, Lena, Justin, LaRee and CherRon waiting for us. Over the loud speakers, we heard Vernel thanking us for taking good care of Lena and welcoming us to their family.

Gloria and Lena wrapped brightly colored blankets around our shoulders. They stood by our side as Vernel asked everyone to join us in the "Honor Dance".

Tears ran down my face. Glancing at Joe, I saw the tears in his eyes. Side by side, with the Sitting Crow family, we walked around the inside of the circle. Everyone came into the circle, shook our hands, stepped behind us, and walked the circle, too. Soon there wasn't anyone on the sidelines. They were all behind us, doing the "Honor Dance". This night is one of our fondest memories.

Joe and I have visited various parts of the world. Normally, after three or four days, I begin to get homesick. Not this time. I wasn't ready to go home. I needed to know more. Something rare, special, and unexplainable had transpired between Lena, the Sitting Crow family and myself. I knew I would not be able to stay away. My heritage was, somehow, connected to Lena and her family.

Not only had I found a new family and friends, I found another me!

I believe the Great Spirit caused the paths of Lena and I to cross. This was not a chance encounter! It was meant to happen!

When we left Red Scaffold, a part of my heart and soul remained.

*" I felt I was leaving
all that I had,
but did not cry."*

Wetatonmi, 1877

# ANSWERS

At home, I constantly thought about what I had seen and felt in the Sweat Lodge. Even today, I only have to close my eyes to be enveloped in the comforting darkness of the lodge. In my mind, I stare into the fire outside the lodge. The faces and eyes are there.

My mind was so full of questions and doubts. I wrote Gloria asking her to discuss with Romanus what I had seen in the fire. I needed to know the meaning of the faces and eyes. When I returned to Red Scaffold a few months later, I learned Romanus' interpretation of the faces and discovered the animal behind the eyes.

The cultural exchange organization collected toys, medical supplies and other items for the people of Cheyenne River Sioux Reservation. Flying to South Dakota to help with the distribution was an opportunity to visit Lena and her family.

Sometimes new experiences seem exciting and different. We often "read" special meanings and feelings into them. These interpretations often disappear when experienced a second time.

I needed to return to Red Scaffold so I could confront what I what I believed happened in my first *inipi*.

As the plane got closer to Rapid City, once again that feeling of "coming home" engulfed me. Seeing Lena and Gloria when I got off the plane increased these emotions.

Normally cold this time of the year (November), the weather was sunny and in the 50"s. As before, I was amazed by the barrenness and the beauty of the landscape.

During the drive to Red Scaffold, Gloria, Lena and I were all talking at once. Excitedly, we told one another of the "happenings" during the past three months.

Gloria told me Romanus was having a "sweat" for me that night. Now I was really excited!

When we arrived at the house, I met Troy. Good looking easy going Troy is going to be a real heart breaker. He greeted me with a big smile and enthusiastic hug. Just as with Lena, Troy and I were instant friends.

It wasn't long before we were talking about Troy visiting New Jersey. Vernel and Gloria told him it depended on his school grades (which were not very good). His grades were much better on his next report card.

As Vernel tells it, Troy casually entered the house, handed his report card to his father, saying, " I'm ready to go to New Jersey ". He had straight A's!

That evening, I changed into my long skirt and tee shirt. I was nervous, apprehensive, and a little scared. Would my response to the second *inipi* be as intense as my first? Had I imagined the visions in the fire? Did I really know the songs? Had my mind fabricated the entire experience?

This time the "sweat" was being held in the lodge at Romanus' home " out in the country ". We went in two cars so all the children could go see their grandparents. I went with Gloria and Lena.

Gloria drove about four miles on the main road, turned left and went about three miles on a road full of bumps, dips, angles, and curves. She stopped to open a large, homemade wire gate, drove through the entrance, then got out of the car again to close the gate. For the next few miles, Gloria told me to watch for cows on the roadway.

Smiling, she said, " It's hard to see black cows at night. "

You would have thought Gloria was a seasoned

race car driver the way she maneuvered that road!

At the top of hill, I could see the lights and the outline of a small house in the valley below. I could see the fire where the sacred rocks were being heated. My nervousness increased. I was clenching and unclenching my cold, sweaty hands. My throat was dry and I could hardly speak.

When we arrived at the house, Romanus and Zona Bear Stops welcomed me ... he with a warm smile and handshake; she with a big hug. The feeling of belonging overwhelmed me again. They were waiting for us to arrive before beginning the "sweat".

Gloria was behind me as I got down on my hands and knees to follow Lena into the lodge. Romanus had entered first, followed by Zona. Vernel entered last. He would assist Romanus. A family friend was the fire tender and would transfer the sacred rocks to the pit. He would open the flap door when needed.

Romanus began singing and praying in Lakota. The others joined in. I listened, silently telling last minute. Each thanked the Great Spirit for His guidance and ask Him to continue to guide and watch over me. I was crying again.

They gave thanks for the love and friendship between us. They spoke of not wanting Lena to go to New Jersey and changing their minds at the last minute.

It was my turn. I was in another world; a world not like today's; a world of unconditional love and acceptance. I heard myself asking the Great Spirit to lead me in whatever direction that would help my new family and friends; to take care of them; and to show me what I could do to help them. I couldn't speak anymore because I was crying so hard. For a while, I don't know how long, I had no control over my thoughts. They just rambled ... unclear ... vague.

*The eyes from the fire ... they're directly in front of mine!*

*I can see widely spread wings! IT'S AN EAGLE!*

Just as quickly, it was gone.

I was back to reality and the ceremony was ending.

*That couldn't be! I didn't hear Zona or Lena pray!*

*Had I been in some sort of trance?*

*How long had my mind been wandering?*

*Did I really see the eagle?*

In their closing prayers, Gloria and Vernel called me "sister". Romanus called me " the soul of a lost daughter come home". We were really family, brought together by an invisible bond of the past and a stronger bond of the present and future.

This time, unless asked, I decided not to say anything about my experience. When we returned to the house, I overheard Romanus speaking to Gloria in Lakota. My name was said several times.

"Did anything happen to you in the sweat", Gloria asked me.

I told her what happened. Romanus smiled and shook his head as he spoke to Gloria in Lakota. A few minutes later, Gloria said it was time to go home. There is no word for "good-bye" in Lakota: and, I knew most Sioux men do not openly show affection. I was really surprised when I reached to shake Romanus' extended right hand and he hugged me with his left arm!

As Romanus hugged me, he said, "You will come home for Sun Dance". It wasn't a request or command, just a statement.

During the ride home, Gloria told me Romanus had seen the eagle in front of me. (I hadn't imagined it!) She then told me his interpretation of the faces and eyes I saw in fire.

" The young girl represents Lena. The profile of the Indian represents the People. Lena brought you to the People. The eyes were those of the eagle, a messenger of the People. You are a messenger of the People ".

Me? Why me? What am I supposed to do? This was difficult for me to comprehend. I seldom understand the reasoning of the Great Spirit. I have learned not to ask questions; just to accept His message and try to follow whatever path He has chosen for me.

*The man who sat on the ground in his tipi meditating on life and its meaning, accepting the kinship of all creatures and acknowledging unity with the universe of things, was infusing into his being the true essence of civilization."*

## Chief Luther Standing Bear

# POWER OF PRAYER

Prayer is the basis of all Native American ceremonies. Their belief in the Great Spirit and all he can do is part of their everyday lives. The prayers and special spiritual ceremonies held by the people of Red Scaffold have helped me through several difficult times. Learning about their lives and participating in the ceremonies has reaffirmed my belief in the power of prayer.

Several months prior to meeting Lena, I had been sick for several months. The doctor said I had Lyme disease. During this time, I was constantly taking antibiotics with little improvement. The doctor was talking about hospitalization and intravenous antibiotic treatments. The week before Lena arrived, a friend told me about a few natural antibiotic herbs. I decided to stop the prescription medications and use the herbs.

When Lena arrived, she called home and ask for " healing prayers " for me. While she was here, I felt terrific..no fatigue, no fever, no joint swelling, or pain. Coincidence? Was it due to the prayers of her family and members of my church, or the herbs?

Since then, there have been many times when

my family and friends on the reservation have held "sweats" and prayed for me. No matter how bad or tired I may feel before going to the reservation, I know I will be physically and mentally revitalized after participating in an *Inipi*.

I believe prayer is the most important medication needed for any illness.

Three years after meeting Lena, I had a another spinal surgery. The surgery went fine. However, Joe was very worried because I was in the recovery room longer then expected.

No explanation was given until I asked the anesthesiologist if I had experienced any breathing problems.

She said, " Yes. Your breathing was irregular. Every few minutes, you would take a few deep breaths and begin breathing normally. This happened several times before your breathing stabilized and we were able to return you to your room."

I was speechless!

I told Joe that, either in surgery or in the recovery room, I had a feeling of being surrounded by a bright, white light. I heard a very gentle, but powerful voice saying, "Breathe Trish. Come on. You can do it. Take a deep breath, Trish".

A week later, Gloria called to see how I was doing. While talking to her, I understood what had happened in the recovery room.

The weather in South Dakota had been too cold for a "sweat" until the morning I went into surgery (Feb.1). On that day, the sun came out and the weather was much warmer. Romanus held a special *inipi* to ask the Great Spirit to watch over and protect me during surgery.

Gloria said, "The presence of the spirits was exceptionally strong."

Everyone knew I would be OK.

While telling her about the bright white light and the voice, we realized they were in the "sweat" the same time I was in the recovery room. My church, also, had prayer chain going for me.

On the reservation, and here at home, everyone calls me "Trish". Was the voice I heard their voices combined into one voice? Or, was it that of the Great Spirit?

" Certain small ways and observances
sometimes have connection
with large and more profound ideas.. "

## STANDING BEAR

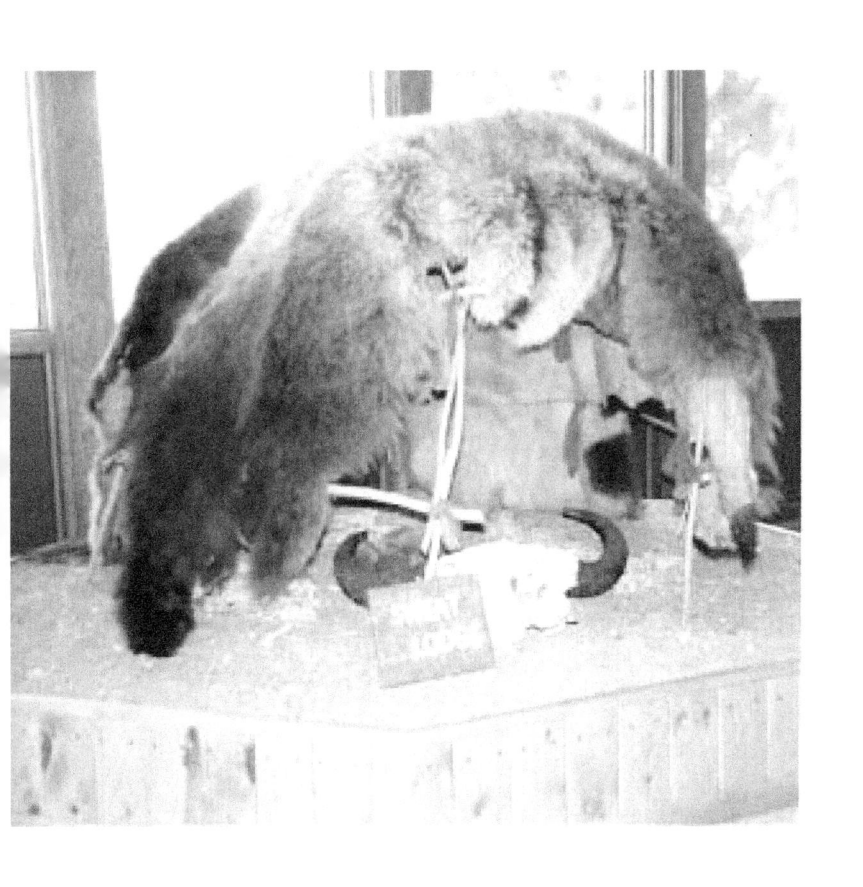

MODEL OF TRADITIONAL
SWEAT LODGE
DISPLAYED AT
BEAR BUTTE, SD

**ROMANUS BEAR STOPS**

# ANOTHER VISIT TO RED SCAFFOLD

Unable to accept fire hydrants without fire hoses, Joe began asking local fire departments for any equipment or firefighting apparel they may be r eplacing. Thanks to the Lafayette Volunteer Fire Dept., Sussex County, NJ, who was getting new items, Joe received coats, a few hats, boots, and 300 feet of fire hose.

In March, 1993, Joe loaded the firefighting equipment in his '87 Ford pickup. He hooked up a donated 28' long, gutted-out travel trailer. We overfilled the trailer with donations of food, clothes and medical supplies. Others who were affiliated with the exchange program had filled another truck with similar items. Joe and another volunteer (driving the other truck) headed for South Dakota. Mary Jo Peer and I flew to Pierre, SD.

Flying into Pierre instead of Rapid City did not take us over the magnificent Black Hills. Not seeing this sacred forest did not diminish the tranquil, yet exciting, feeling of "coming home". Once again, seeing Gloria, Justin, and CherRon when we arrived at the airport reinforced these unexplained feelings. Friends of Mary Jo's were there to meet her.

Joe was pulling into the driveway when we arrived at the Sitting Crow home. Tired from the long drive, he was happy to see our friends again. The Sitting Crow children and many of their friends gathered outside the trailer to see what "goodies" he had brought. Romanus and Zona Bear Stops, Roy and Molly Circle Bear, and a few others were there to greet us. It was an emotional "family" reunion.

We had a lot to do in the three days we would be here. We had to meet the other truck in Eagle Butte the next morning to help unload both trucks. The items were to be distributed by Tribal Council and the Senior Citizen Center coordinators. Before going to Eagle Butte, we had to unload special articles for the Sitting Crow family and people of Red Scaffold.

There was a special gift for Lena's family. Lena, Troy, and Vernel knew what it was. With Vernel's help, Joe removed the item from under the bags of clothing in the truck. It wasn't heavy, just awkward. Gloria was asked to stand in front of the trailer door with her eyes closed.

Her look of surprise and happiness when she opened her eyes and exclaimed "A microwave!' was priceless.

We unloaded boxes of M&M's, Skittles, Combo's, cookies, crackers; plus, dishes, cooking utensils, soap, and a couple of IBM typewriters. We were exhilarated seeing how much happiness these items brought to everyone.

Later, Joe found Zona Bear Stops typing away on the typewriter given to Gloria. That's when we learned Zona had worked for many years with the senior citizens on Rosebud Reservation (SD). One of her ambitions was to write down many of the stories of her people. (Unfortunately, Zona went to live with her ancestors before writing her stories.) The next morning, Joe removed another typewriter from the trailer. That evening we took it with us when we went to visit Romanus and Zona "in the country".

When we arrived at their home, I went in the first. I asked Zona to sit at the kitchen table and close her eyes. Joe carried the typewriter in the house and sat it down in front of her. When she opened her eyes and saw the typewriter, you would have thought she found a $100. She said it was the one thing she wanted and thought she would never get. Joe and I were overjoyed at being able to fulfill this unknown wish.

The next morning we headed to Eagle Butte. Mary Jo met us there. The items unloaded from the trucks amazed those watching: wheelchairs, walkers, crutches, medical supplies, clothing, food, toys, etc. They could not believe the donations we had received. Their expressions of gratitude was all the thanks we needed.

That afternoon, Joe met with Vernel and three Red Scaffold men for a three-hour firefighters training class. He explained the "buddy system" when entering a burning building, staying low to the floor, avoiding a "back draft", and other firefighting basics. Joe suggested they hold classroom demonstrations in the school for the children while wearing their firefighters gear. He explained how, in the midst of smoke and flames, a small child often perceives an approaching firemen as a "monster". If this happens, the child may hide from the fireman, resulting in unnecessary injury or death to the child or fireman.

Following the class, the men unloaded the firefighting equipment and tried on the firefighter jackets and hats. Vernel was designated "Chief" of the " Red Scaffold Community Volunteer Fire Dept." Of the five working fire hydrants in Red Scaffold, two are on the main community road, one near the Sitting Crow's garage where the equipment was stored.

The number of firefighting articles Joe collected is minimal compared to what is needed. We pray Red Scaffold never has to use the equipment . They still need fire fighters gloves, hats, boots, and more hoses. Fire and firefighting equipment are nonexistent in most communities.

Once again , Romanus honored me by asking me to participate in a "sweat". Although somewhat skeptical, Joe went, too. Knowing how much I am effected, he wasn't sure what to expect. Not liking extreme heat, he was only able to endure an hour or so. *Inipi's* can last one to three hours or more.

Joe's experience was not dramatic, but he now understands the spirituality of the *inipi*. As for me, I once again found myself singing and feeling like I was were I was meant to be.

Spiritual experiences do not happen to everyone, nor do they happen each time. When they do happen, you do not question what you may have seen, heard or felt. You just accept it.

*" Yesterday I heard something that made me almost cry. "*

*Little Wound (Cherokee)*

Zona Bear Stops

**GERMAINE SITTING CROW**

*" Sometimes we prayed in silence; sometimes each of us prayed aloud; sometimes an aged person prayed for all of us...."*

# Geronimo

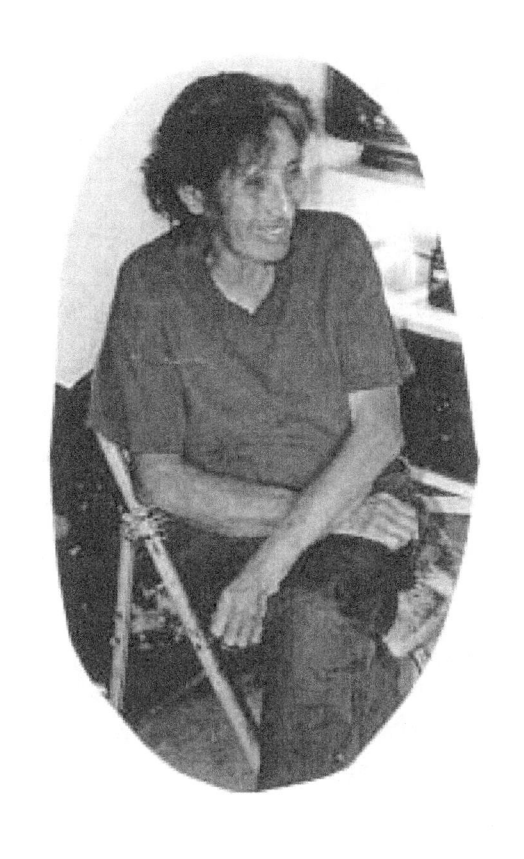

MOLLY CIRCLE BEAR

# EAGLES

On one of my unexpected visits to Red Scaffold, Molly Circle Bear said, " You are like the eagle. We never know when or where you will land or how long you will stay."

Most Native Americans believe everyone has an animal spirit that is part of their persona. I believe mine is the eagle. Since discovering the "eyes" in my first *inipi* were those of an eagle, I have often seen eagles (real and in dreams) when and where least expected.

When I am feeling "low" or facing a difficult situation, an eagle appears in the sky, in a picture, or in a dream. That's when I think of Molly. She is watching over me. A smile comes to my face. I know whatever the reason for my "down and out" mood, everything will be OK. The Great Spirit and the eagle watch over me and those I love. Together they will guide me in the right direction.

While dancing on the sidelines and looking towards the top of the ceremonial tree at my first family Sun Dance, I saw a giant eagle. Seeing eagles flying overhead during a Sun Dance is normal. However, I learned later, the eagle had only been seen by Vernel (who was dancing) and myself.

That night, while sitting by the sacred fire, Vernel told me the eagle had been sent by the spirits to welcome me. I felt very honored and humble.

On another visit, Mary Jo Peer and I spent a few days on Pine Ridge Reservation, in the Badlands. With a small group from New Jersey, we visited Bear Butte, the site of sacred Indian burial grounds. We climbed to the top and gave tobacco offerings to the Great Spirit.

After a physically and mentally exhausting, but great day, eight of us got into the van for the drive back to Pine Ridge. I was driving. Mary Jo was in the passenger seat. The others were dozing in the back.

We were on the road that goes through the Badlands, not far from Pine Ridge Reservation.

*Suddenly!!!*

*From nowhere!!!*

*An Eagle!!!*

It swooped down from the sky and, for a few seconds, seemed suspended in midair directly in front of the windshield.

Just as quickly, it was gone.

I was so tired, I thought I was seeing things. I looked over at Mary Jo.

She turned to me and said, "I saw it, too."

The summer of '94, Vernel and Gloria chaperoned 15 children to New Jersey. I was really surprised when Romanus and Zona Bear Stops got out of one of the two vans. They had come to "check up on me". (I'd had another back surgery and was unable to go to Sun Dance.)

The group was performing at a local powwow and had brought their ceremonial attire. Vernal had the sacred eagle staff used during Sun Dance and other ceremonies. We hung the eagle staff from an upstairs rafter in my home.

I live in a small rural town, on a lake in northwest New Jersey. There are mountains, lakes and a lot of wooded areas. Eagles are not a common sight.

Within a short walking distance of our home is a small wooded mountain overlooking the lake. This became known as "Romanus' Spot" because he went there to pray.

One afternoon, he and I were sitting on a rock at "his spot" when he casually looked up and pointed out three eagles circling above us. He told me the Great Spirit had sent them to watch over me.

(Silently, I wondered if they had followed the eagle staff from South Dakota.)

On the day the group left for home, I found a small eagle feather on my deck.

Romanus said, "It is a thank you gift from the Great Spirit."

Romanus tells me the Great Spirit shows me eagles as a reminder that he is watching over me.

Could he be right?

*The good road and the road of difficulties*
*you have made me cross;*
*and where they cross*
*the place is holy."*

## Black Elk

BADLANDS, SD

BEAR BUTTE

MARY JO PEER GIVES TOBACCO OFFERING TO THE GREAT SPIRIT AT THE TOP OF BEAR BUTTE.

*House made of dawn...*
*restore my feet to me...*
*Happily I recover...*
*my interior becomes cool*
*As it used to be...*
*I walk in your beauty.*

## NAVAJO PRAYER

# RELIGION & *WIWANYAG WACHIPI* (SUN DANCE)

The Sun Dance is one of the most religious and spiritual Native American ceremonies . It is, also, the most misunderstood. (Sun Dance was banned by federal statue in 1886. It was legalized in 1934.)

Religion, as defined by Thomas J. Sullivan and Kenrick S. Thompson in "Sociology: Concepts, Issues & Applications", is a "collectively held set of values and rituals that express a basic understanding of the world, especially the sacred dimension; and the ultimate concerns of the meaning of human existence"

Native Americans trust in a creative power that is higher than all people and the universe. Each tribe calls this Great Spirit by a different name. To the Lakota (Sioux), he is Wakan T'anka. The God of Native Americans is eternal, having no beginning and no end. He provides mankind with a never-ending life after death.

In "Mystic Warriors of the Plains: The Culture, Arts, & Religions of the Plains Indians", Thomas E. Mails says "the only difference between religion of Native Americans and Christians is: The Indian came by divine providence to know the same God as the Christian; but, he knew Him only in an abstract way, leaving him to wondering and superstition. The informed Christian knows the will of God through Christ and the books of the Bible."

Just as Christians incorporate sacred ceremonies into their worshipping, Native Americans have special ceremonies to honor the Supreme Being. Of the seven rites of Native Americans, the "Sun Dance" is the most misinterpreted. This ceremony seems barbaric to some people because of the piercing ritual.

In "The Sacred Pipe: Black Elks Account of the Seven Rites of the Oglala Sioux", Black Elk talks of Sun Dance, a four-day ceremony held during the first full moon in June, and the significance of two eagle bones being pierced through a man's chest or back to which a single leather thong is attached. The thong is then connected to the tree in the center of the sacred circle. Dancers participate in a traditional ceremony, pulling the eagle bones from the flesh.

Native Americans who participate in the Sun Dance believe everything comes from the Great Spirit. All they have to offer in thanks is a piece of their own flesh. They pray that their people may walk the holy path of life.

The sacred cottonwood tree that serves as the Sun Dance alter is often referred to as " that man in the middle". It is believed the cross on which Jesus was crucified was made from a cottonwood tree. aaccording to Black Elk,d one of the reasons for using the cottonwood tree is because of the perfect five-pointed star revealed in its grain when an upper limb is cut crosswise. This "star" represents the Great Spirit

Is the symbolism of the cottonwood tree that is prayed to at Sun Dance any different then Christians praying to a cross in church?

Many Christian revivals include singing, dancing, and praying. These revivals normally last several days. The Sun Dance is an annual four day ceremony of prayers and thanksgiving to the Great Spirit and to all the powers between those of earth Wakan T'anka.

Personally, I see very little difference between Sun Dance and a Christian Revival.

Sun Dance, the *Inipi*, and other Native American ceremonies meet Sullivan and Thompson's definition of religion. Aren't these ceremonies entitled to the same acceptance?

The Sun Dance arbor is always circular as it represents all creation. Twenty-eight poles, representing the sacred numbers 4 and 7 (4 x 7 = 28) are used to build the arbor.

2 for the Great Spirit
2 for Mother Earth
4 for the Four Winds:
    East, South, West, North
1 for the Sacred Spotted Eagle
1 for the Sun
1 for the Moon
1 for the Morning Star
4 for the Four Ages of Man:
    Face of the Child, Face of the
    Adolescent, Face of the Adult,
    Face of the Aged
7 for the Seven Sacred Rites
1 for the Buffalo (who has 28 ribs)
1 for the Fire
1 for the Water
1 for the Rocks
1 for the Two-Legged People

(War bonnets usually have 28 feathers. And the moon only lives 28 days.)

The number 7 represents the Seven Sacred Rites, excluding the *Sacred Pipe Ceremony*:

    ***Inipi***: Sweat Lodge Ceremony
    ***Hanblecheyapi:*** Crying for a Vision
    ***Wiwanyag Wachipi:*** Sun Dance
    ***Hunkapi:*** Making of Relatives
    ***Otuha***: a Give Away Ceremony for the
             Keeping of the Soul;

***Isna Ta Awi Cha Lowan***: Preparing a
    girl for Womanhood.
***Tapa Wanka Yap***: Throwing of the Ball
    (Today the game represents the course
    of a man's life, which should be spent
    trying to get the ball which represents
    Wakan T'anka)

There are seven symbols honored when preparing your pipe: the four directions (east, south, west, north), Mother Earth, Father Sky, and the Great Spirit.

The number 4 represents the:

    4 races of man:
        red, yellow, black ,white
    4 directions:
        north, east, south ,west
    4 things that breathe:
        those that crawl, those that fly,
        those with two legs and those
        with four legs
    4 things above the earth:
        sun, moon, stars and planets
    4 parts of plants:
        roots, stems, leaves, fruits or flowers
    4 divisions of time:
        day, night, moon, year
    4 elements: fire, water, air, earth
    4 tribal principles:

      Respect for Wakan T'anka
      Respect for Mother Earth
      Respect for our fellow man
      Respect for individual freedom

Even the human heart has four compartments.

The sacred cottonwood tree in the center of the arbor represents Wakan T'anka, the Great Spirit. Everything comes from the Great Spirit and everything returns to Him.

I have had the honor of participating in several Lakota ceremonies including the *Wiwanyag Wachipi, Inipi, Hunkapi,* and *Otuha.* Many were held at the sacred family grounds of Romanus Bear Stops where "Sun Dance has been since
the beginning".

My participation in these spiritual ceremonies has reinforced my belief in many unexplainable forces that are "out there", and that the Great Spirit (God) is the most powerful of all.

*" When we lift our hands*
*we signify our dependence*
*on the Great Spirit. "*

BLACKFOOT

SUNDANCE TIPI'S
&
SWEAT LODGE

# MY FIRST SUN DANCE

Mother Earth tried to absorb the rain as fast as it came down, but with little success. Her deep, dry crevices and trenches seemed to strangle her as her thirst for water was quenched. The rain fell through the night. Her surface quickly turned to thick mud.

The thunder that roared over the barren plains sounded like giant bowling balls being thrown down an endless alley. Lightning flashed. The sky looked as it were being lit with millions of miniature fluorescent lights. The seven-year drought had ended.

This was the first night at Bear Stops family Sun Dance. Joe, Margaret (his mother), and I had arrived early Friday afternoon, the second day of Sun Dance. We had driven from New Jersey, towing a 20-foot trailer full of food, clothing, and other donated items for the people of Red Scaffold. When we arrived that afternoon and approached the top of the hill, we had our first look at the Sun Dance grounds.

The view was breath taking and calming at the same time. The Sun Dance tree stood tall in the center of the arbor, ablaze with colored "flags" waving in the breeze .... red, yellow, black, brown, white, green, blue. (The tobacco offerings, wrapped in colored cloth, had been tied to the tree branches prior to the raising of the tree by families and friends requesting special prayers.) We could hear the drums and the singing. To the right of the arbor, surrounded by a stockade fence were two tipis and two sweat lodges, one for the women dancers and one for the men.

In front of the tipis, the sacred fire burned. It had been lit Wednesday, when the sacred tree had been raised.

My skin tingled as I felt the spirituality of this very sacred ritual. We parked behind the house. We were greeted with love and friendship by family and friends. I felt that familiar feeling of "coming home".

After the hugging and handshaking, we began to unload the trailer and sort all the items: men's, women's and children's clothes; food, paper items, toys and "goodies" for the children. Once again, we were impressed by the dignity and thoughtfulness of the people as they helped one another choose items each could use.

Soon it was dinner time. Joe and I hungrily looked forward to eating fry bread. During Sun Dance, lunch and dinner is served buffet style. Breakfast is generally cereal, eggs, and bread. Lunch is sandwiches of peanut butter and jelly, Spam, and luncheon meats. A delicious *wahanpi* (stew of meat and vegetables or macaroni), cake, and fry bread are served at dinner. Everyone, except the dancers, snack throughout the day. (The children love large kosher dill pickles.) The food is donated by those attending Sun Dance. The women share the cooking and cleanup.

The last day of Sun Dance is the traditional "feast day". (The first day is "tree day" followed by four days of ceremonial dance and praying.) Stew is prepared. There is a smorgasbord of donated foods including salads, vegetables, fry bread, cakes, and *wojapi* (a delectable, pudding-type dessert usually made with blueberries).

Margaret's pure white hair peaked the interest of the children. (She was 78 years young,) It wasn't long before they were all calling her "grandma". She was like the Pied Piper. Children followed her everywhere. Margaret also spent a lot of time with the older women, sharing craft ideas, recipes, and stories.

Joe and I went for a walk in the surrounding fields. That's when I found my "*wotai*". According to many Native Americans, Mother Earth has a special stone to give to everyone. You just have to recognize it when she presents it to you.

While walking up a hil in the surrounding fields,I spotted a white quartz stone, about two inches square, lying by itself. When I picked up the stone, I noticed what appeared to be a spot of blood on it. Upon examining it further, I realized the stone, when held sideways, looked like an eagle's profile. The "blood spot" ingrained into the stone was the profile of a bear.

Amazing when you remember I was at the Romanus BEAR Stops family Sun Dance in RED Scaffold. Excited about my find, I showed it to Zona Bear Stops. After examining it and holding it tightly in her fist, she said "It is very old. Many spirits live in this stone. It is your *wotai*. Keep it always."

Today, I keep it in a special medicine pouch. Each time I have been in the hospital, it has been with me. Sometimes, when I hold it in my hand I can feel it giving me strength for whatever is happening in my life.

That evening, as dark clouds gathered in the sky, and the rain began, everyone began preparations for the night. Those who lived nearby left for home, while others went to their tents and vehicles. We headed for the truck. Joe and I would sleep in the back and his mom would sleep on the front seat. (Good thing she's short.) Being tired from the long drive and an exciting day, we all immediately fell asleep.

A short time later, we were awakened by the raging storm. The rain pelted Mother Earth while the thunder roared and lightning lit up the Father Sky. It was the most exhilarating, frightening, and beautiful storm I had ever seen.

I thought about the sacred fire. It must not go out!

I remembered the two men dancers who were fasting and sleeping within the sacred circle; they will be soaked.

I worried needlessly. The Great Spirit watched over the dancers and the fire did not go out.

Strange? Maybe. Anything is possible within the sacred circle. (I have never understood why the sage, used for the boundary of the sacred circle, never blows away regardless of how fierce the wind may be.)

Walking in the mud the next morning was like trying to walk in Vaseline a foot deep. Mud was everywhere, except inside the arbor. The ground there was wet, but not muddy.

The sacred fire had not gone out. The dancers, according to what I was told, had huddled under their blankets, pressing their bodies close to Mother Earth. She kept them dry.

We were awaken at sunup to the singing and praying of Romanus Bear Stops. The dancers entered the sweat lodges for a purification ceremony and to pray for strength. Once they have entered the sacred circle, they will dance till sundown with only occasional rest breaks. I was invited to take part in the *inipi* even though I was not dancing.

The spirituality and bonding of one with infinitywas overwhelming. That feeling stayed with me the rest of my visit.

As I danced under the arbor, outside the sacred circle, with my Lakota family and friends, I felt myself being drawn back into that "other world". A world where everyone and everything are a part of one another. A world of harmony. A world of love and forgiveness.

It's hard to explain. I was consumed by the wonderful feeling of unity with Mother Earth and the Great Spirit.

*"The Great Spirit is looking at me and will hear me."*

CHIEF JOSEPH

*"The man who sat on the ground
in his tipi meditating on life
and its meaning,
accepting the kinship of all creatures
and acknowledging unity
with the universe of things,
was infusing into his being
the true essence of civilization."*

Chief Luther Standing Bear

# HEALING CEREMONY

The last day is a special day. A healing ceremony takes place and flesh offerings are made to the Great Spirit. Romanus announced it was time for those needing special healing prayers to enter the sacred circle. Vernel and Lena stood on either side of me. They guided me to the sacred tree. Gloria and LaRee did the same with Joe.

Entering the sanctity of the sacred circle was like entering a holy place that evil could not penetrate. We placed our hands on the tree, bowed our heads, and began to pray. Each dancer stopped behind those at the sacred tree and prayed for us. They touched our heads, shoulders, and backs with their hands and eagle fans.

My hands were flat against the tree.

I could feel life in the tree … blood pumping through veins … a heartbeat within.

I was one with the Great Spirit!

When I left the sacred circle, I knew I was free of the Lyme disease that had plagued me the past year. I was refreshed, energetic, and at peace with myself.

The Great Spirit, God, or whatever name you call the Supreme Being, had touched me. I felt a peaceful, yet, electric inner glow that I was sure everyone could see in my eyes.

*"Great Spirit, once more
behold me on earth
and hear my feeble voice"*

## Black Elk

# *FLESH OFFERING*

Women dancers and those who are not dancing ... men, women, children ... may give a flesh offering to the Great Spirit. The sacred pipe is held as the Sun Dance leader, using a small surgical knife, pricks skin from their shoulder, and places it in a red cloth. (Red represents the color of Life.) Sage is used to stop the bleeding. When everyone has given their offering, the Sun Dance leader prays as he ties the red cloth to the sacred tree.

I watched intensely, as the men dancers prepared for their flesh offerings. They stood in front of the sacred tree, holding the sacred pipe, looking towards the sky. Vernel made two small incisions on each side of their chest. An eagle bone was inserted through one incision and out the opposite cut. One end of a piece of rope was tied to the ends of both eagle bones. The other end was already attached to the sacred tree.

The drums began.

Prayer songs were being sung as they prayed with their hands on the sacred tree.

The men began to move away from the sacred tree.

> *BACK* ... ..stretching the rope ... praying....
>
> *FORWARD* ... to the sacred tree ... touching the tree ... praying ...
>
> *BACK* ... *BACK* ... stretching the rope more ... praying...
>
> *FORWARD* ... to the sacred tree.. touching the tree.....praying...
>
> *BACK* ... *BACK* ... *BACK* ... stretching the rope even more ... you can see their skin stretching ... the eagle bones are beginning to pull from their skin.

There is a look of tranquility on their faces.

They appear to be oblivious to the present time.

They participate in this historic ritual to honor all mankind, hoping their offerings will make a difference in their lives and the lives of others.

> *FORWARD* ... one last time... wrapping their arms around the sacred tree ... praying.
>
> *BACK* ... *BACK* ... *BACK* ... *BACK* ... stretching the rope till the eagle bones tear from their skin.

As the eagle bones are torn from the dancers chests, an eagle is souring above. You can here his call. Is he acknowledging their prayers?

Many of the women begin the traditional musical expressions made by clicking their tongues. The spirituality of the moment is over powering.

The dancers leave the sacred circle. Bystanders line up to shake their hand to thank them. It is a traditional bonding of understanding, love, hope, and thanksgiving. We all share tears of gratitude for their sacrifice.

## *MITAKUYE   OYASIN!*

*" There is one God looking down on us all.*
*We are all children of one God..*
*God is listening to me.*
*The sun, the darkness, the winds,*
*are all listening to what we now say. "*

## Geronimo

MARGARET (JOE'S MOM) HUGGING LAREE, DANIELLE (TRICIA'S DAUGHTER), LENA, & TROY

# VISITS TO NEW JERSEY

When Joe drives to the "rez" during the summer, he always comes home with additional passengers.

The summer we drove to Red Scaffold for our first Sun Dance, Lena and Troy returned to New Jersey with us. They were asleep, on mattresses in the back of the truck as we traveled east on Interstate 80. Troy woke up as we were approaching the Delaware Water Gap (entering NJ from PA).

Troy shook Lena awake, screaming, "Look out the window! Look out the window!"

Both were excited about "all the green trees".

Arriving at our home on Cranberry Lake, they appeared a little scared. This changed with their first plunge into the lake. It wasn't long before they made friends and were joining in the basketball games at the beach club.

The following year Joe drove and I flew out. When he was ready to leave for home, Gloria called Joe aside. She told him LaRee had packed her suitcase and told her, "I'm going to sneak into the back of the truck, curl up like a little ball and hide under something. Joe won't find me till its too late to turn back."

Lena and Troy put their things in the truck. Joe asked Gloria and Vernel if he was forgetting anything.

LaRee stood by the truck, looking at Joe with big puppy-dog eyes. Pretending not to notice her, he said they had to leave, " And if anyone else can pack their suitcase and be in the truck in two minutes, they can come, too."

LaRee ran in the house, grabbed her suitcase, and jumped in the back seat. Everyone was laughing. Joe told her she could go as long as she made his sandwiches.

Her smiling face beamed as she screamed, "OK!".

Not long after leaving Red Scaffold, Joe stopped at a grocery store to buy sodas, snacks, and items to make sandwiches. The kids told Joe they liked "ham and cheese". Each time he picked up a pack of ham and a pack of cheese, they said it was the wrong kind. Finally, Joe told them to get the kind they wanted. They showed him "ham and cheese", ham imbedded with cheese nuggets. The kids laughed at being able to "pull one over on Joe".

The summer Romanus and Zona came with the group from Red Scaffold, we were able to show them things they had only dreamed about. Neither of them had ever been to the East Coast.

Joe took Romanus and Vernel fishing on his 28' boat. They went from the Atlantic Highlands, NJ, area to the ocean. They cruised pass New York and the Statue of Liberty. Romanus could not believe he was seeing the Statue of Liberty and the Atlantic Ocean. Zona and I took long walks in the wooded area near our home. She found flowers and plants that once grew in South Dakota, some she had not seen since she was a little girl. She told me stories of how her ancestors had used them for medicines.

Our visits to see our family and friends living in Red Scaffold , and theirs to see us, are precious, unforgettable memories for all of us.

Each time, I look at the many photos I have taken over the years, I thank the Great Spirit for bringing Lena into my life. Had we not met, I would not have this wonderful, loving, extended family.

" We see the changes of day and night ..
the seasons, the stars,
the moon, the sun.
Anyone must know
it is the work of someone
more powerful than man."

## Chased-By-Bears

LENA SITTING CROW
JULY, 1990

CHERRON & LAREE SITTING CROW
POCONO RENAISSANCE FAIR
VILLAGE OF CANTERBURY, PA

TROY SITTING CROW
FISHING OFF THE TIP OF
SANDY HOOK, NJ

LAREE, LENA, TROY SITTING CROW
CRUISING PAST NEW YORK SKYLINE

**JUSTIN SITTING CROW
6 YRS OLD
"POW WOW TIME"**

TOM ROME
(TRICIA'S SON)

# RETURNING FOR SUN DANCE

I missed Sun Dance the following year. I found out later that Lena had given a flesh offering in my honor. Was that why she was in my dreams every night of Sun Dance? In these dreams, she was wearing a Sun Dance dress and shawl, holding the sacred pipe as her father accepted her flesh offering. Separated by over 2,000 miles, I felt her love and concern for me.

The following year, I gave a flesh offering and danced on the last day. I thanked *Wanka T'anka* for the prayers, love, and friendship of Lena, my Lakota family and friends.

The week prior to Sun Dance, Gloria called and told me a special ceremony would be held after Sun Dance.

*Romanus Bear Stops was going to adopt me!*

*I was going to be his daughter!*

Surprised, all I could do was cry tears of love and happiness. To receive this honor by such a respected Lakota elder is an honor rarely given to a *wasicu*.

Tom Rome (my son), Mary Jo Peer, and I arrived on tree day. We would be there to place our prayer ties on the sacred tree. (Mary Jo and I made tobacco ties on the plane.) We would participate in the traditional tree raising ceremony.

When our plane landed in Rapid City, I knew another new dimension was about to be added to my life. That "coming home" feeling was even more prevalent when I spotted Gloria, Lena, CherRon and Justin waiting to welcome us.

A mysterious ribbon of the past and present was going to be knotted, binding us permanently together for eternity.

Mary Jo and I were extremely excited, apprehensive, and feeling very humble because we would be dancing on the last day of Sun Dance .

Tom would assist with the sacred fire.

I seemed to be in some sort of trance as I thought what it meant to be adopted by Romanus.

Joe was driving to the reservation, towing a large trailer full of food and gifts for the Sitting Crow family and friends. He arrived two days later.

On Tree Day, we watched as a hole was dug in the center of the sacred circle for the tree. Sage and tobacco were placed in the hole. The ropes for the men's flesh offerings were tied to the tree's branches. A prayer was said before everyone tied their tobacco offerings on the tree. Then a group of men lifted the tree while others guided the tree into the hole. Amazing!

The next three days, Mary Jo and I spent most of our time dancing in place, closely observing the dancers and listening intently to the singers and drummers. We ask questions as we tried to learn as much as possible before Sunday morning, the last day of Sun Dance.

Saturday afternoon, I was watching the dancers, totally engrossed in the spirituality of the ceremony and oblivious to my surroundings. My arms were raised towards the heavens, giving thanks to the Great Spirit. I was looking towards the top of the sacred tree, at the clear blue sky.

*What's that hovering above the sacred tree!*

*A huge eagle glistened in the sunlight!*

I was so startled, my arms dropped to my sides, tapping Zona Bear Stops on her shoulders.

I turned to Mary Jo and whispered, "Did you see the eagle?".

She gave me a strange look and nodded, "No".

Was my imagination working overtime?

Sitting by the sacred fire with Vernel and Gloria that evening, I told them about the eagle. I explained how the eagle looked like fine crystal as it soared on wings spanning at least ten feet. It glistened in the sunlight. Hearing myself describe the eagle to them I realized I must have imagined it. That's when Vernel told me he had seen the eagle, too.

Wow! I shared a vision with the Sun Dance leader!

I told Vernel I wanted to give a flesh offering to thank Wakan T'anka for his guidance and healing. We decided he would take seven small pieces of flesh from my right shoulder, forming a feather.

Why a feather?

I didn't know then. Now, I believe, it bonded me with the eagle.

*" We may quarrel about
things on earth,
but we never quarrel about
The Great Spirit. "*

## Chief Joseph

# DANCING AT SUN DANCE

In preparation for participating in the dancing , Mary Jo and I had made long, ankle-length, chemise style dresses with three-quarter length sleeves, from cotton calico type material, We gathered sage and wrapped it with material scrapes; then, shaped the finished pieces into crowns for our heads and bands for our wrists and ankles.

We would be dancing with Lena, LaRee, Gloria, Zona Bear Stops, Molly Circle Bear (Gloria's mother), Germaine Sitting Crow (Vernel's mother) and several friends, including a dozen men. The dancers were not only from Cheyenne River Sioux Reservation, but from Colorado, California, and other areas of the U.S. Vernel was the Sun Dance leader. Romanus Bear Stops and Roy Circle Bear would join the singers and drummers.

There was electricity in the air!

At sunrise, Mary Jo and I made our way down the hill to the sweat lodge. Outwardly, we appeared confident. Inwardly, each of us was a nervous wreck. Scared of doing something wrong and a little afraid of experiencing the unknown, we barely spoke.

It was time to enter the women's sweat lodge for purification and prayers. A strange, calming feeling came over me. Everything was as it should be. I was with family and friends who were a part of me.

Immediately following the "sweat", we entered the tipi with the other dancers. We changed into our Sun Dance dresses. Outside the tipi, we grouped together, assisting one another as we wrapped fringed shawls around our waists. Molly Circle Bear had lent a shawl to Mary Jo. Zona Bear Stops gave me one of hers. Gloria lent us pipes and instructed us on how to fill them.

Kneeling in front of the fire, we took small amounts of the tobacco and sage mixture. Each time, before putting it into the pipe, we said a silent prayer ... first to the each of the four directions; Mother Earth; Father Sky; and then to the Great Spirit. Once filled, the pipes were placed on a rack made of tree branches. The men were doing the same. All was quiet and still. It was a time of reverence.

*Listen!*

*Hear the drums!*

*Hear the singers!*

It's time to start.

We formed a single line, men first. I glanced at Mary Jo, standing behind me. We exchanged brief smiles of encouragement and reassurance. A special bond of friendship and love was created between the dancers. For those who had danced together before, the bond was reinforced. The procession to the arbor began.

Vernel was in front carrying the sacred buffalo skull and eagle staff.

Tom (my son) brought the smudge pot (burning sage and cedar) to each of us so we could complete our purification before entering the sacred circle.

Fanning the smoke from the smudge pot into my face was rejuvenating. As I waved the smoke into my face and lightly around me, I felt myself being transported to a time I knew little about, but felt I belonged.

We entered the sacred circle from the east. Standing at the entrance, raising my arms to each of the four direction before entering the circle, I stepped back the past. A time that, I knew, was connected to my past, present, and future.

The day stretched into intervals of an hour or more of dancing, separated by 20-30 minute rest periods. Dancing, singing (how did I know the songs?), and holding our pipes up as a symbolic offering to the Great Spirit (how did I know when to raise my pipe), we were transported back to a more reverent time, a time of our ancestors.

When we left the sacred circle through the west opening, we raised our hands and looked towards Father Sky as we paid homage to the four directions. Each time we left the sacred circle, we stood our pipes side by side on a tree branch rack, touched the sacred buffalo skull, and caressed the sacred eagle staff. I felt an inner peace.

The number of "rounds" during Sun Dance depends on the number of dancers. Each dancer has a pipe that must be lit and smoked till the tobacco is gone. At the end of each "round", one or more pipes are handed to someone waiting at the south opening. The pipe is handed from the dancer to the recipient four times before being accepted. The pipe is passed among the drummers, singers, and others on the sidelines to smoke until empty. The pipe is then carried back to the south opening and given back to the owner in the same way. The Sun Dance leader escorts the owner to the rack and the pipe is placed on the opposite side of the rack. When all the pipes have been passed around and smoked by onlookers, the day's dancing is over.

During the rest periods, men and women rest in

separate areas of the arbor. Lying on my blanket, I wondered why I wasn't completely exhausted? Why doesn't my back hurt;? Why are there no blisters on my bare feet? Why am I not thirsty?

Except for occasional sips of chokeberry juice, we were not allowed to eat or drink till after the "*inipi*" at the end of the day.

During a midday rest period, I saw Vernel standing at the sacred tree praying. Others were forming a line outside the west opening. It was time for the flesh offerings. Joe and Tom watched as I got in line. They looked surprised, but proud. I knew they believed in me and accepted whatever I may do.

*The line is getting shorter.*

*Only one person in front of me now.*

*Can I do this without flinching? Without tears?*

*My turn....*

I faced Vernel as raised my hands and I turedn to honor the four directions.

Vernel offered me the pipe four times. The fourth time, I accepted the pipe.

Vernel smiles and stepped to my left.

As I hold the pipe with both hands, I looked towards the top of the sacred tree, silently praying to Wakan T'anka.

Vernel is making small incisions in my left shoulder, taking seven pieces of flesh as he shapes the feather. (I had asked him for the feather as we sat by the sacred fire the night before.)

I feel nothing except the love of the Great Spirit and the People.

An image of an eagle appears in the sacred tree.

## *MITAKUYE OYASIN!!!*

*" I feel glad as the ponies do
when the fresh, green grass
starts in the beginning of the year. "*

## TEN BEARS

## AND NOW.....

Tears stream from my eyes as Zona ties the small shell, adorned with four eagle feathers, into my hair.

I am now the proud daughter of Romanus Bears Stops and the sister of Gloria Sitting Crow.

My Lakota name is:

>"CHAN TE' WAS TE' WEN"
>*(Good hearted Woman)*

I pray I will be able to live up to my new name and the expectations of my new family, friends, and the Great Spirit.

## *MITAKUYE OYASIN!!!*

TRICIA AND HER NEW LAKOTA PARENTS
ROMANUS & ZONA BEAR STOPS

JOE, TRICIA, GLORIA, ZONA, & ROMANUS

*MITAKAYE OYASIN!*

*ALL MY RELATIONS!*

# UPDATE...

Over the years, several friends have visited the reservation with Joe, Tom, and I.

Lorna Colwell went to a Sun Dance and became friends with Angelina, a quiet young girl who spoke very little and could not tell time. By the end of our visit, she was talking and Lorna had taught her to tell time. (Lorna sent her a watch for Christmas.)

Since my adoption by Romanus Bear Stops (June, 1993), Mary Jo and I have danced at three Sun Dances and participated in several "sweats" and other ceremonies.

Tom is still a "fire man" for the sacred fire. Vernel presented him with an eagle feather at a Sun Dance.

Joe and I continue to receive donations of items for the people of Red Scaffold. We visit them whenever possible.

It's hard to believe that Lena is 22 and has a one year old son, Sun Dance Sitting Crow, born June 16, 2001 (during Sun Dance). His Lakota name is " *Wanbli Ahipi Hoksila* ", which means, " Eagle Brought Him ".

With the help from many who care, Lena went to college for two years. She now manages the Red Scaffold Youth Center and hopes to be able to return to college someday for her teaching degree.

Gloria is a director with Head Start in Eagle Butte. She is still actively involved with the people of Red Scaffold, helping whenever and wherever she can.

At the June, 2001 Sun Dance, in a special ceremony, Vernel became "Chief Sitting Crow".

Romanus continues to be a significant part of my life. I love talking to him and listening to his stories. I hope to record his life's story; and, I pray at each Sun Dance to see him there the following year. His presence is an important link to the past.

Zona Bear Stops and Molly Circle Bear have crossed over to reside with their ancestors. There are many times when I feel their presence and know they are watching over me.

Troy lives in Minneapolis, MN, where he works as a "tin cutter" for a company that builds airplanes.

Jennifer lives in Denver, CO, with her two girls, Elena and Suzanne.

CherRon and LaRee are in high school. Both dance at powwows and Sun Dance.

Justin is 12, plays baseball and likes to fish.

Two of my grandsons, Joseph and Robert Cibula, have gone to Sun Dance with me. Robert did a special project on Sun Dance for his school's 7th grade "Cultural Day. (He got an "A".) On Robert's second visit to Sun Dance, he impressed Germaine Sitting Crow by being able to speak a little of the Lakota language.

Life on the reservation is still much the same. The interest in their culture and ceremonies is increasing. Each year, I see more young people at Sun Dance. Fire trucks and emergency equipment are still needed. Many still struggle to feed and clothe their families.

Each visit to the "rez", I still experience that feeling of "coming home". When returning to New Jersey after a Sun Dance or " *Inipi* ", I am more in touch with the "inner me" and the Great Spirit.

The compassion and courage of my family and friends living on Cheyenne River Sioux Reservation is evident in their everyday life.

I am honored to be considered "one of the family".

*MITAKUYE OYASIN !!!*

*" So it is with Wakan T'anka.
We believe that he is everywhere,
yet, he is the spirit of our friends,
whose voices we cannot hear."*

## CHASED-BY-BEARS

CHIEF VERNEL SITTING CROW

# A SPECIAL GIFT

Sun Dance, June 2000, marked seven years since my adoption by Romanus. Joe, Tom, and Mary Jo were there. Joe helped where needed. Tom was the "fire man" watching over the sacred fire. Mary Jo and I danced the last two days.

The day before Mary Jo and I were to dance, we gathered sage for our crowns, wristbands and ankle bands. The prairie was "green". Wildflowers bloomed everywhere and the sage was tall and plentiful. Water was flowing in Cherry Creek. It was beautiful!

Not having a pipe, we each had to borrow one. Friday evening. I went to the house to borrow a pipe from Gloria. I found her in the bedroom making her sage crown and bands. She was dancing the last two days, too. Justin and CherRon were helping.

When I asked Gloria about borrowing a pipe, she told CherRon to ask Romanus, Vernel, Lena, and LaRee to come into the bedroom. They had completed the evening "sweat" and were resting outside. It wasn't long before they all came in the small bedroom, closing the door behind the them.

Gloria removed a package, about 15 inches long and eight inches in diameter, from the top of a tote bag sitting in the corner.

Together, she and Lena handed it to me saying, "We love you."

Sitting on the bed, I slowly unwrapped the package. I had no idea what was inside, but I knew it must be something very special.

Under the brown paper was red material wrapped around an object. As I unwrapped the red material, I was in a state of disbelief.

Feelings of honor, love, pride, happiness, and amazement sent chills down my spine. I could not believe what I saw.

Their gift to me was the most sacred of all gifts....

My own ...

## *SACRED PIPE !!!*

# MITAKUYE

# OYASIN !!!

*"Friends and relations...*
*You know what I feel...*

## WAWATAM 1763

VERNEL & GLORIA SITTING CROW

JUSTIN SITTING CROW

CHERRON SITTING CROW

JENNIFER SITTING CROW

LAREE SITTING CROW

AUGUST, 2002

***Listen to your inner voice ...***

Guidance comes in dreams,

Quiet times,

From the actions of others,

The words of our elders,

In prayer .....

***Listen to your heart.***

## DONATIONS

Please send donations for distribution (blankets, bed linens, towels, coats, jackets, jeans, toys, baby & food items) to:

>Gloria Sitting Crow
>Red Scaffold # 644
>Faith, SD  57662

The Andover Presbyterian Youth Connection starts **a Christmas Toy Drive on November 1.** For more information contact:

>Rev. Kathy Jamoury
>Andover Presbyterian Church
>Route 517
>Andover, NJ  07821
>973-786-5094

For other information, please contact:

>Tricia Sedivy
>265 Route 206
>Andover, NJ  07821
>email:  triciased@aol.com

Together we can make a difference in the lives of people living in Red Scaffold, Cheyenne River Sioux Reservation, SD.

Joe Sedivy

# ABOUT THE AUTHOR ...

Tricia Sedivy has always felt a connection to her Native American heritage and something "spiritual out there". As a child, she would visit her grandparents in Cosby, TN. That's when the feelings were always very strong. Growing up in Baltimore, MD, she searched for answers by attending various churches, and reading books on religion, spirituality, and native American cultures.

Tricia was in her mid-40's when she became involved with an American Indian exchange program and the Lakota people living on Cheyenne River Sioux Reservation, SD. This was the beginning of her unexplainable relationship with Lena Sitting Crow and the Sitting Crow family.

She has a special love for the people living in the community of Red Scaffold. With the help of her Lakota family and friends, Tricia has learned more about herself and her heritage. This knowledge has helped her to accept, without question, the spirituality of what is "out there".

Tricia resides with her husband, Joe, in Byram Township, NJ. Both visit Red Scaffold whenever possible. In an effort to make more people aware of the life and traditions of the Lakota on Cheyenne River Sioux Reservation, she is always eager to speak to schools and organizations about the "rez".

# BIBLIOGRAPHY

"Sociology: Concepts, Issues, & Applications" (2nd Edition); Thomas J. Sullivan & Kenrick S. Thompson, MacMillam Publishing Co.

"Mystic Warriors of the Plains: The Culture, Arts, Crafts & Religions of the Plains Indians"; Thomas E. Mails,The Mallard Press, 1991

"The Sacred Pipe: Black Elk's Account of the Seven Rites of the Oglala Sioux"; Recorded and edited by Joseph Epes Brown; Penquin Books, 1981

"Mitakuye Oyasin: We are all related"; Dr. A. C. Ross (Ehanamani) Bear Publishing, 1992

"Mother Earth Spirituality, Native American Paths to Healing Ourselves and Our Worlds"; Ed McGaa (Eagle Man); Harper Collins Publishers, 1990

"A Cherokee Feast of Days, Daily Meditations", Joyce S. Hifler, Council Oak Books, 1992

"Ghost Dance"; David Humphreys Miller; First Bison Books, 1985

For additional copies of

**"Spirits & Eagles"**
(Ask about discount for quantity purchases.)

Or

**Information regarding Tricia
Speaking to your organization**

Contact:

**Tricia Sedivy**
265 Route 206
Andover, NJ 07821

**triciased@aol.com**

*MITAKUYE OYASIN !!!*

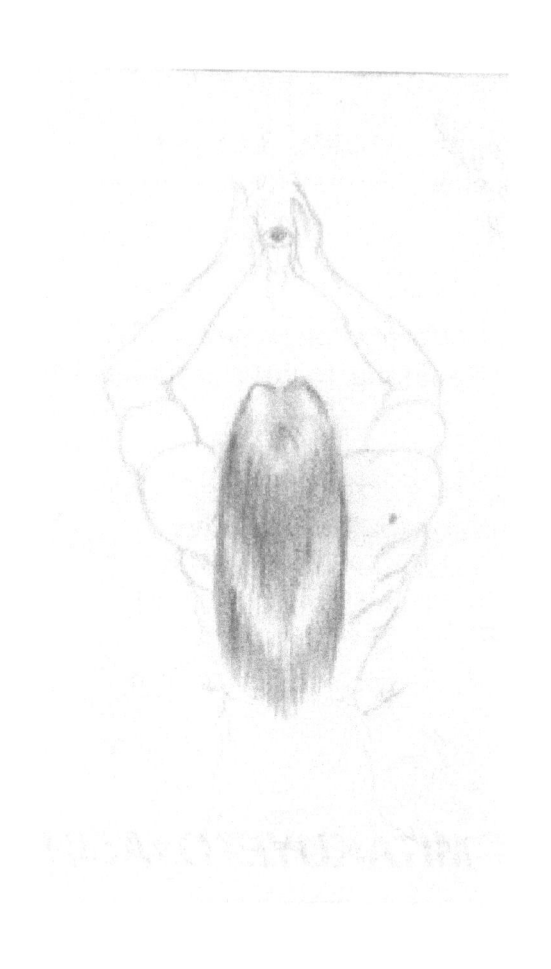

DRAWING BY

VERNEL SITTING CROW

*May the Great Spirit
watch over you and yours.*


*Tricia Sedivy
Chan'te' was te' wen*

Made in the USA
Middletown, DE
27 July 2024